WA...
ABEL TASMAN
COAST TRACK

P H I L I P   H O L D E N

Hodder Moa Beckett

By the Same Author

New Zealand Non-fiction
Pack and Rifle
Hunter by Profession
Backblocks
The Deer Hunters
Seasons of a Hunter
The Hunting Breed
On Target
The Wild Pig in New Zealand
The Golden Years of Hunting in New Zealand
The Golden Years of Fishing in New Zealand
New Zealand: Hunters' Paradise
Holden on Hunting
The Deerstalkers
A Guide to Hunting in New Zealand
The Hunting Experience
Hunt South
Wild Game
More Holden on Hunting
Fall Muster
On the Routeburn Track
In Search of the Wild Pig
Station Country
Always Another Hill
Wild Boar
Holden's New Zealand Venison Cookbook
Station Country II

Pack and Rifle (1995 edition)
Great Hunting Yarns
The Way of a Hunter
Station Country III
New Zealand Hunter
A Backcountry Journey
Walking the Routeburn Track
The Milford Track Adventure
50 Great Farmstays in New Zealand

Young Adult Fiction
Fawn
Stag
White Patch
Razorback

Children's Fiction
Lucy's Bear

Children's Non-fiction
Sheep Station

Australian Non-fiction
Outdoors in Australia
Along the Dingo Fence
Crocodile
Wild Pig in Australia

Front cover photo: Onetahuti or Tonga Beach by Gareth Eyres, Exposure.
Back cover photos: On the Coast Track (left) and Tinline Bay (right) by Philip Holden.
Map: Terralink.

ISBN 1-86958-815-0

© 2000 Original text and photography — Philip Holden
The moral rights of the author have been asserted.

© 2000 Design and format — Hodder Moa Beckett Publishers Limited
Published in 2000 by Hodder Moa Beckett Publishers Limited [a member of the Hodder Headline Group],
4 Whetu Place, Mairangi Bay, Auckland, New Zealand

Produced and designed by Hodder Moa Beckett Publishers Limited
Colour separations by Microdot, Auckland, New Zealand
Printed by Toppan, Hong Kong

Acknowledgements

I AM GRATEFUL TO Abel Tasman National Park Enterprises for letting me make full use of its facilities while I carried out the field research for this book. In particular, I'd like to thank Darryl Wilson and his helpful office staff at Motueka.

Afield, in a pleasing mixture of weather conditions that allowed me to photograph the Coast Track in a variety of moods, I enjoyed the company of guide Geoff Button, whose knowledge of everything to do with this region, and its flora and fauna, and Maori history and customs, might well be unsurpassed. We're never too old to learn something new, and in my particular case Geoff proved this was true.

Once again on this project, I found Department of Conservation personnel to be especially helpful and I make special mention of Rudy Tetteroo, Motueka, and Brendon Clough and Helen Campbell, who are based at the Nelson office.

Thanks are also due to Liz Boot of the Awaroa Lodge and Café.

Philip Holden
September 2000

Contents

Introduction

THE ABEL TASMAN NATIONAL PARK covers 22,530 hectares of mostly hilly-to-mountainous country lodged between Tasman Bay and Golden Bay at the top of the South Island. It is the smallest national park in New Zealand. The Abel Tasman Coast Track itself is far and away the most popular and easiest to traverse of all of the Department of Conservation's 'Great Walks'.

This wonderful coastline is perhaps unsurpassed anywhere in the country. Here are sweeping beaches with golden sands, secretive little coves, sheltered bays, rugged headlands and intriguing offshore islands. The Coast Track also wanders through mixed manuka and kanuka scrubland and splendid stands of native forest. It crosses

Left: Trampers heading north across Onetahuti Beach towards Awaroa.

Below: On Stilwell Bay — across the Astrolabe Roadstead lies Adele Island.

'bridged' streams, rivers and estuaries, where it is subject to tidal flows; and, in places, it offers fine views of the heavily-forested hinterland. By trail's end, the Coast Track is an experience you will reflect upon with a deep and lasting pleasure.

Unlike the Milford and Routeburn tracks, which close because of snow, the Abel Tasman Coast Track can be walked all year round. In fact, many people prefer to tackle it in autumn and winter when the track is less crowded and there is an invigorating sharpness in the air. While the overall climate here is mild, it is best to remember that on winter nights it can be chilly.

Left: These independent trampers, walking the Coast Track from Totaranui, are crossing the Bark Bay stream.

Below: Awaroa estuary at low tide — the boys are fishing for whitebait.

General Information

THE ABEL TASMAN COAST Track can be walked from two directions — from the south (Marahau) to the north (Wainui Carpark), or of course the other way around. Either way it is 50 km of undemanding walking. Most trampers tend to take 3–5 days to complete the full length of the Coast Track. Those trampers who cut out the northern section of the walk — Totaranui to Wainui Carpark — make their walk a three-day one. They might start their walk at Marahau or Totaranui, and might begin or conclude their Abel Tasman Coast Track adventure with a launch trip to or from Kaiteriteri. The launch service is used by both independent and guided walkers and is operated by Abel Tasman National Park Enterprises. Personally, I consider a sea trip along this spectacular coastline a must.

The Abel Tasman Coast Track can cater for a wide variety of visitors. Many people, such as family groups who are slowed down by children, prefer to walk certain legs of the track rather than tackle the entire walk. Such a tramp between bays might take a few hours of easy walking, or perhaps longer if they intend to have a picnic and a swim and sunbathe. Other trampers might follow this basic principle but be a little more adventurous. For example, Abel Tasman Coachlines offers one-day excursions among a number of attractive packages for those with a limited amount of time to spare.

For example, you can catch the coach to Kaiteriteri or Marahau and board the boat to cruise to Torrent Bay (4 hours' walk) or Bark Bay (6 hours' walk). You can leave the boat at either bay and walk back to Marahau — experiencing the best part of the track on the way. Coaches depart from Marahau at either 3.30 p.m. or 5.30 p.m. to return to Nelson.

Sea-taxi operators also provide the same sort of service. (Refer to page 55 for Sea-transport Options.)

Sea kayaking is extremely popular along this coastline, as the region is New Zealand's premier sea-kayaking destination. Some visitors will kayak a certain section of the coastline, such as Marahau

Left: Kayakers in Stilwell Bay.

to Torrent Bay, and walk the rest of the track. They tend to think they are getting the best of both worlds. Certainly no other Great Walk in the country, or even a major tramping track, can offer the visitor such a wide array of options.

The already-mentioned Abel Tasman Coachlines, which is based at Nelson, provides a complete service to all parts of the Abel Tasman National Park. This service is linked for convenience with InterCity Coachlines operating between Picton, Nelson, Christchurch and the West Coast.

Abel Tasman Coachlines operates a bus from Nelson through to Richmond, Mapua, Tasman, Motueka, Takaka, Wainui Carpark and Totaranui once daily. The total trip to Totaranui takes approximately four hours. At the time of publication, its bus leaves Nelson at 7.20 a.m. Buses run three times a day from Nelson, Richmond, Mapua, Tasman, Motueka and Marahau.

For more information, please contact:
Abel Tasman Coachlines
Nelson Telephone: (03) 548-0285
Motueka Telephone: (03) 528-8850
E-mail: atc@nelsoncoaches.co.nz
Website: www.nelsoncoaches.co.nz

Track Accommodation

THERE ARE FOUR DEPARTMENT of Conservation (DOC) huts and 21 campsites on the Abel Tasman Coast Track. The huts' capacities at 2000 and 2001 are The Anchorage with 28 bunks and gas cooking, Awaroa with 22 bunks and gas cooking, Bark Bay with 28 bunks and a wood stove, and Whariwharangi with 20 bunks and an open fire.

The huts contain bunks, mattresses, heating, toilet facilities and access to water — but they do not include cooking equipment so trampers are advised to carry a cooking stove.

Left: Observation Beach is just one of 21 campsites. A kayaking party appears to have set up camp near the campsite sign. The best feature of a boat trip along the coastline is that it allows you to view it from a completely different aspect.

Camping is restricted to established sites. The advantages of staying at designated campsites are that they have a fireplace, toilet and access to water. Designated campsites are found at Tinline Bay, Apple Tree Bay, Akersten Bay, Observation Beach, Watering Cove, Te Pukatea Bay, The Anchorage, Torrent Bay (two sites), Bark Bay (two sites), Mosquito Bay, Tonga Quarry, Onetahuti, Awaroa, Waiharakeke Bay, Totaranui, Anapai Bay, Mutton Cove and Whariwharangi Bay.

Trampers need to book during the summer season: 1 October to 30 April. The bookings desk is open from 1 July for the forthcoming season. The peak season is from 20 December to 31 January. At other times of the year, a 'first come, first served' system applies.

Below: Roughly 27,000 people will stay at Bark Bay Hut each year.

For information about hut and campsite tariffs, please contact:
Abel Tasman Coast Track Bookings Desk
c/o Motueka Information Centre
Wallace Street, Motueka
Telephone: (03) 528-0005
Fax: (03) 528-6563
Website: www.motueka.net.nz

Another point to note is that Giardia has been found in park waters. Giardia is a parasite, invisible to the naked eye, which can cause severe stomach illness. Take no chances. You can kill Giardia cysts by bringing drinking and cooking water to a fast boil for 3 minutes or by treating with an additive available from pharmacies or from DOC offices. A filtered-water supply is available at Totaranui and the Department of Conservation huts at The Anchorage and Bark Bay.

DOC would also like to inform visitors that it runs a Safety Watch free phone: 0800 999-005, which is to be used in the case of an emergency. The department will follow up any safety concerns.

Totaranui Campground

THE TOTARANUI CAMPGROUND IS operated by DOC, it can cater for up to 800 visitors, and frequently does, at peak holiday times. The name Totaranui means 'many trees'. It was first mapped in 1865 as Gibbs Station. Totaranui is 32 km east of Takaka and it is reached via a narrow, winding road where driving with caution is advised.

The DOC office is located in the visitor centre, where there is a filtered-water supply, a public telephone, notice-boards, orientation maps and a schedule of bus and sea-transport options. There are two boat ramps at the northern end of the beach. Totaranui is an ideal spot for swimming, diving and water-skiing.

The DOC office is staffed from Labour Weekend (the third weekend in October) to early December on a Monday to Friday basis, but from then on, it is staffed seven days a week until early March. The centre remains open all year round so that trampers can check in and check out.

A canteen is open during the summer season. Among the variety of items on sale that trampers may have overlooked are insect repellent (sandflies can be especially troublesome), Coast Track hut and campsite passes, sunscreen, candles and gas canisters. A small range of foodstuffs and drinks is also available — but no bread or milk.

For information about Totaranui Campground, please contact:
Department of Conservation
Takaka Field Centre
PO Box 53
1 Commercial Street, Takaka
Telephone: (03) 525-8026
Fax: (03) 525-8444

Please note:
Over the peak season from 20 December to 31 January, it is advisable to book to ensure a place.

Below: The DOC Information Centre at Totaranui.

Awaroa Lodge and Café

ACCOMMODATION, MEALS, COFFEE AND tea — or something stronger — can all be found adjacent to the Coast Track at Awaroa Lodge. Backpacker accommodation for seven people is also available. The main lodge is located about 300 m from the sea and is considered an ideal base or stopover point for independent trampers wanting the luxury of hot showers and prepared meals. Guided walks and guided kayaking trips — especially those catering for first-time kayakers — are also available. Awaroa Bay and its immediate surroundings are wonderful for watching birds, swimming, sunbathing and just relaxing. Each year around 8000 people take advantage of what Awaroa Lodge and Café have on offer.

Below: Awaroa Lodge's backpacker accommodation (pictured) is not to be confused with Awaroa Lodge, located nearby.

Awaroa Lodge and Café can be reached on foot from Totaranui or Marahau, or by launch or sea-taxi, or even by air with Tasman Bay Aviation (there is an airstrip near the lodge). Just 1 hour's flight from Wellington, or 20 minutes' flight from Nelson could have you touching down in a subtropical wonderland you might never want to leave.

For more information on Awaroa Lodge and Café, please contact:
Awaroa Lodge and Café
PO Box 163
Takaka 7172
Golden Bay
Telephone: (03) 528-8758
Fax: (03) 528-6561
Website: www.awaroalodge.co.nz

Please note:
Awaroa Lodge is closed during the winter season.

For more information about flights, please contact:
Tasman Bay Aviation
Telephone: (03) 547-2378

The Guided Walk

IF YOU DON'T WANT to walk the track independently, Abel Tasman National Park Enterprises provides another option. It operates on the track — either way — between Marahau and Totaranui. The total package includes guides, food, equipment, a combination walk and kayak trip, two first-class lodges right on the coast (complete with chef) and sea-transport on its own launch at the start or end of your walk. (Refer to page 60 for more details.)

Right: A party on the guided walk crosses the swing-bridge on the Falls River — the most scenic river on the Coast Track.

Landforms

SOFT SEPARATION POINT GRANITE is the predominant rock in the area the Coast Track passes through. It is the explanation for the characteristic shape of the land that was formed following the Ice Age of about 14,000 years ago. The infinitely slow breaking-down of the granite landmass, further eroded by the sea along the actual coastline, is apparent in the texture and appearance of the reddish-brown or near-white beaches. They have been called '. . . the finest small beaches in the country' and few could argue with that.

The vegetation also reveals the largely unproductive nature of the soils that develop on granite — this is even more apparent after the burning-off of the original forest cover. A telling example of this vegetation can been seen on the exposed headland that the Coast Track traverses before the track drops down to The Anchorage.

The slightly acidic taste of the water in rivers and streams is also a direct result of granite soils. The brown, tea-like colour that occurs in some streams is caused by tannins, leaf litter and humus.

Along the Coast Track, and adjacent to it, are six estuaries. They are at Marahau, Torrent Bay, Bark Bay, Awaroa, Totaranui and Wainui. They have complex and fascinating ecosystems. Many birds inhabit the estuaries because of the food sources that are readily available to them there: fish, shellfish, snails, crabs and worms.

Below: A typical granite rock coastline south of Totaranui.

Native Birds

BY THE TIME YOU'VE taken full advantage of what the Abel Tasman Coast Track has to offer — including its coastline — you will have encountered a diversity of bird habitats. These range from low-lying forest, scrub, rivers and estuaries, swamps, lagoons, beaches and offshore islands. As a result, the birdlife is far more diverse than it is on any other of the Great Walks in the country — and therein lies a part of the Coast Track's enormous charm.

Among the birds you may see and hear in low-lying forest are the bellbird, tui, native pigeon, South Island robin, grey warbler, brown creeper, fantail, rifleman, kaka, morepork, tomtit and weka.

The track's swamps and lagoons, rivers and estuaries, beaches and offshore islands are the home for a variety of other birds. These include black, spotted and pied cormorant, black-backed, red-billed and black-billed gull, white-fronted tern, kingfisher, blue penguin, pied and variable oystercatchers, grey duck, pukeko, Australasian gannet, pied stilt, white-faced heron, white heron and banded dotterel.

Note: While the white-faced heron is included, it is not a native bird, having arrived from Australia in the late 1930s and early 1940s. However, it is the most common heron in the country today.

Another interesting import, seen around the Marahau wetlands and elsewhere, is the Canada goose.

Top: The flightless weka was a ready source of food for Maori and, later, European settlers.

Second from top: Tui are often seen along the track.

Centre: The pukeko favours a swampy habitat.

Second from bottom: Pied cormorants are common along the coastline of the Abel Tasman National Park.

Bottom: Variable oystercatchers are readily observed in and around Awaroa estuary.

Other Wildlife

FUR SEALS INHABIT THE Adele and Tonga Islands. They are found on the mainland at Separation Point, which is reached by a side-route off the main Coast Track. While there is an established year-round colony of seals here, the main concentrations are found in the winter when the adult and young males arrive from breeding grounds in the south.

Dolphins may also be observed from time to time along this coastline.

Introduced Animals

ACCORDING TO DOC SOURCES, trampers on the Coast Track see red deer and wild pigs only 'very occasionally'. Sightings of these animals and feral goats are more common in the higher and much wetter hinterland. Possums are widespread throughout the Abel Tasman National Park.

APPROXIMATELY 30,000 TRAMPERS, EITHER independent or on guided walks, are to be found each year on the Abel Tasman Coast Track. Of this number, less than 10 per cent complete the entire walk — that is, including the northern section between Totaranui and Wainui Carpark. DOC views this as disappointing as this northern leg of the Coast Track has much to offer, with a detour to Separation Point arguably being the highlight.

Collectively, as many as 175,000 people visit this coastline each year. Whether they are trampers, kayakers, day-trippers, boaties, caravanners, or whatever, I doubt that any of them will be disappointed with what they find here. Truly, the Abel Tasman Coast Track is the sparkling jewel in the Nelson region's crown.

History

PERHAPS MORE THAN 800 years before the arrival of the European in New Zealand waters the Maori had already discovered the coastline of the Abel Tasman National Park. This was a subtropical region blessed with a mild climate and long hours of sunlight.

Both the sea and land proved bountiful for this race of hunter-gatherers. Fish and shellfish abounded, whitebait swarmed in estuaries and eels slithered in streams and rivers. The starch-rich roots of the bracken fern contained a source of carbohydrate essential for their overall health and the earth was fertile enough for them to grow kumara, the sweet potato. Flightless birds were simple to hunt and even some birds with the power of flight, such as the native pigeon, were easily taken.

The first people to have arrived here from the North Island are thought to have been the Ngaitara. As likely as not they had been driven off their land by inter-tribal warfare. They established a number of permanent and semi-permanent settlements along the coastline. Permanent settlements on the Coast Track are thought to have been at

Above: A profusion of driftwood on the raised sandy ground above Onetahuti.

Above: Looking north along Onetahuti or Tonga Beach as it is also known.

Awaroa, Torrent Bay and Apple Tree Bay, among other places. They lived a simple life-style — which might have lasted indefinitely had not fate dictated otherwise.

It would seem that all went well for the Ngaitara until about 1600 when the superior forces of the Ngati Tumatakokiri tribe took control of the coastal regions of the Abel Tasman National Park in a series of battles.

On 13 December 1642, the Dutch seafarer Abel Janszoon Tasman, then exploring the previously uncharted waters of the Southern Hemisphere, sighted the West Coast of New Zealand. In two ships — the *Heemskerck* and *Zeehaen* — he sailed north.

Tasman's logbook records that on the evening of 18 December, his ships dropped anchor somewhere west of Separation Point. The commonly-held belief was that they dropped anchor near the Tata Islands; however, it is more likely to have been off Whariwharangi Bay (included in the northern section of the Coast Track). It would also appear that the Dutchmen had already observed camp-fire smoke near the beach.

After dark, four Maori canoes put out to sea. However, they only came so far. Loud voices called out to the Europeans but, of course, they were not understood. Then one of the Maori began to blow on what sounded like a Moorish trumpet. An officer on the *Zeehaen* replied in kind — a musical interlude that served no purpose at all. Soon the Maori canoes returned to shore.

At dawn the next morning, the *Zeehaen*'s cockboat, carrying seven men, crossed to its sister ship so that the officers could consider the situation. Were the natives friendly or otherwise?

Meanwhile, there was much activity on shore.

By the time the cockboat was making its return journey to the *Zeehaen*, eight canoes had ringed the two ships. Isaac Gilsemand, the artist on board the *Heemskerck*, drew a sketch of this incident which shows that the 'praus' — double canoes — may have held up to 11 men.

Suddenly the leading canoe rammed the cockboat and by spear or club four Europeans were killed. The surviving Europeans desperately swam for safety while the Maori were quickly driven off in the face of a volley of gunfire from the *Heemskerck*.

Tasman saw no good reason to linger. But even before they weighed anchor, an even bigger war party, this time in 11 canoes, was heading towards them at a great rate of knots. But the Maori had no answer to a sustained volley of gunfire from both ships and swiftly drew back out of range. Tasman would name this place Murderers' Bay. (It later became Golden Bay.)

In 1828, Te Rauparaha combined the forces of several tribes and ended the long occupation of the Abel Tasman coastline by the Ngati Tumatakokiri. The Ngati Tama, Te Atiawa and Ngati Rarua became the new occupiers. To this day they remain the tangata whenua (people of the land).

The various names of places — bays, streams and so on — in this region are a colourful mixture of Maori, French and English. The French connection is linked directly with Dumont D'Urville, who, in January 1827, anchored his corvette, *Astrolabe*, between the mainland and Adele Island (this strait is now named the Astrolabe Roadstead). In stark contrast with Tasman's experience many years previously, the Frenchmen were given a warm welcome by the local inhabitants.

For a week, D'Urville's team of scientists explored the country between Torrent Bay and Marahau. They gathered plant specimens and wrote detailed accounts of whatever they found of interest. In the meantime the crew, after having had a rough time crossing the Tasman Sea, replenished their water and wood supplies, and took advantage of any local produce that was offered.

Significantly, the maps of this coastline that were subsequently drawn up by D'Urville proved far superior to those drawn by either Tasman or Captain James Cook, on whom D'Urville had openly modelled himself. Taking this into account, perhaps the name of this Frenchman — rather than that of a Dutchman who, disgruntled with Maori hostility, did not even set foot in New Zealand — should have been perpetuated in the naming of New Zealand's smallest national park?

European settlement came to this region in 1855, when William Gibbs settled at Totaranui and Ambrose Ricketts settled at Awaroa.

Above: Fisherman Island was named by D'Urville.

At Totaranui, Gibbs established a farm that he called the Totaranui Estate. While at Awaroa, Ricketts built sailing vessels — an industry would continue there for about 50 years.

It would become a regular thing for ships to anchor off the beach at Totaranui, where they would replenish supplies of fresh water and farm produce (such as meat, milk, butter, eggs and vegetables).

Meanwhile, a vibrant sawmilling industry was progressing, with sawmills having been established at Totaranui, Waiharakeke and Awaroa. The logs were transported from where they fell to the sawmills by either bullock teams or tramways. Stone was also quarried for building near Arch Point and many farms were established. By 1870, another boat-building operation was under way at Frenchman Bay, and Torrent and Bark Bays were settled at about that time. The area was serviced entirely by sea.

Above: Late evening at Awaroa, with the tide out.

Gradually, however, the large-scale devastation of the forest reaped its inevitable results: most of the valuable timber, especially rimu and kahikatea, was gone. So sawmills closed, and when the workforce moved on, there weren't enough children to keep schools open. Many of the farms were abandoned. The main reason for this was the poor quality of the land itself, but land access was also difficult. Wild pigs, which preyed on stock and destroyed crops, were something else the early farmers had to contend with. (It is on record that Totaranui Estate was completely fenced to keep out wild pigs.)

By the early-to-mid-1930s, only a few diehards remained, but, in the meantime, a number of holiday homes had been built in various parts of the coastline — setting a future trend.

The Abel Tasman National Park was established in 1942 and the often-voiced fears that future logging would destroy the now-revitalised forest vanished like a puff of smoke on a windy day.

The year 1992 not only marked the 50th birthday of the Abel Tasman National Park, but also the 350th anniversary of Tasman's visit. A number of events were held in celebration — the most significant being a visit by Queen Beatrix of the Netherlands to look upon the Abel Tasman Memorial at Tarakohe and to meet with the tangata whenua. This was a wonderful occasion noted for the genuine respect that two great races of seafarers and settlers held for each other.

Left: In the early morning: two trampers from Israel skirt the estuary near the DOC hut at Awaroa. They are en route to The Anchorage hut.

The Abel Tasman Coast Track

THE MOST SIGNIFICANT ASPECT of the Abel Tasman Coast Track is that it is so completely different to other well-known tracks such as the Milford or Routeburn tracks. For instance, the Coast Track essentially hugs the coastline and there are no gutbusting climbs to overcome. The Coast Track is also so well-graded and maintained that heavy boots can be cheerfully left at home — and what joy it is to bounce along a forest trail in nothing more than lightweight running shoes!

Above: Looking down on Torrent Bay and the estuary of the Torrent River at high tide. At such times, trampers use the alternative track around the inlet.

Left: The cascades of Simonet Creek.

Day One:
Marahau to The Anchorage and Torrent Bay

MARAHAU MEANS 'GARDEN OF the world'. This peaceful spot is 67 km from Nelson and 6 km north of Kaiteriteri. Located on the western shore of Tasman Bay, Marahau is often referred to as 'the Abel Tasman Village'.

At the first sweeping glance, Marahau appears to consist mostly of privately-owned holiday homes. Time seems to have stood still or barely moved at all here. This might be the New Zealand of a much earlier era. But this is the Abel Tasman Village and visitors are well catered for. At the Marahau Beach Camp, there are sites for caravans, campervans and tents. The Barn at Marahau offers various types of accommodation while more upmarket accommodation can be found at Ocean View Chalets and the Abel Tasman Marahau Lodge. There is also a motor camp.

Old Macdonald's Farm, a 402-ha leisure park, offers secure vehicle parking. Free parking can be found at the DOC carpark near the park entrance. Several kayaking and sea-taxi companies are based here too.

The Park Café and Restaurant is located near the DOC Information Shelter, at the park entrance. The DOC shelter has a display of interesting aspects of the park and this is where the Coast Track begins.

The track between Marahau and The Anchorage and Torrent Bay is well-graded and mostly follows the route that was known as the 'Settlers' Track'. But firstly, by way of a wooden-planked walkway, you cross the broad estuary of the Marahau River — a wetland area rich in birdlife. The source of the river rises close to the highest point in the Abel Tasman National Park at Mount Evans (1156 m).

The introduction to the Coast Track itself is unfortunately the least rewarding aspect of the day's walk — for it traverses country where the results of over-logging and fires are clearly seen: hillsides are rampant

Right: The beach at Tinline Bay.

with gorse, while radiata pines stand tall among scrub and bracken: but it gets better.

Tinline Bay is reached after less than an hour's walk, and the scenery is beginning to improve. The bay was named after John Tinline, an early settler. There is a large campsite above the beach and picnic tables.

The 'Tinline Nature Walk' starts at the campsite. In a looped fashion, lasting about 30 minutes, it takes you to a stand of native forest that is typical of what this coastline was like before the arrival of the European. There are also similar stands of native forest further on.

Presently a small stream, rushing pell-mell between moss-coated rocks and boulders, is crossed via a bridge. It must have caught D'Urville's eye because he named it Simonet Creek, after one of the sailors who was with him at the time.

Soon Fisherman Island can be seen. It was also named by D'Urville. The island is said to be free of predators. The larger Adele Island, named after D'Urville's wife, is nearby. D'Urville named the beach here The Big Beach and wrote of it: '... it is the pleasantest spot on the whole coast and the richest in birdlife'. Later, European settlers planted apple trees here and it became known as Apple Tree Bay. There is a campsite here.

Stilwell Bay is reached in a short time. It is named after the Stilwell family of Motueka who, in the late 1920s, built a holiday home here. From the beach, you look out to Adele Island.

There is also another DOC campsite at Akersten Bay — named after William Akersten, a prominent settler of Nelson. Nearby Yellow Point is so named after the profusion of yellowish lichens that grow there.

From here the Coast Track heads inland, although at no time is it at any great distance from the sea. I enjoyed this part of the first day's walk very much because of several deep and damp gullies where rimu, matai, miro and, among other trees, the odd kahikatea — the tallest of the tall — all stand. Tree-ferns are abundant and streams and creeks chuckle away in gully bottoms. Birdlife is very evident — if not always

Right: Kayakers at Stilwell Bay. Adele Island is in sight, and, on the skyline across Tasman Bay, lies Nelson's coast.

in sight, then, almost always, in sound. This is the New Zealand forest as it was meant to be. Beyond an exposed granite headland, rampant with only the hardiest of scrub growth, lies The Anchorage — the most sheltered, all-weather anchorage along this coastline. The Anchorage hut (containing 28 bunks) and campsite are located here. The hut is the first (or last) DOC hut on the Coast Track.

Several marked walks can be made from The Anchorage. For example, a roughly 45-minute tramp across the granite headland will take you to Watering Cove (where there is a campsite). The crew of the *Astrolabe* replenished their supplies of fresh water and caught up on their washing in this lovely little spot.

At the northern end of the beach at The Anchorage, the Coast Track cuts up and over a small headland and then drops into the watershed of the Torrent River. Torrent Bay was named by D'Urville because of 'the three lovely torrents which run into it'.

Below: The beach at The Anchorage; the calm waters of the bay offer a safe harbour for all manner of boats.

Marahau → 4 hr
Anchorage ↓ 5 min

The inlet here can be crossed with safety within 2–3 hours of low tide; otherwise, use the track around the inlet. Beyond the inlet are a DOC campsite and the guided walkers' accommodation at Torrent Bay Lodge.

There are two worthwhile walks from Torrent Bay. The first is to Cleopatra's Pool — a 30-minute walk around the back of the inlet and left of the river to an excellent swimming hole.

The second is to Falls River — a 2–3 hour walk past Cascade Falls before reaching the river (the falls are about 15–20 minutes upstream).

Below: Torrent Bay Lodge.

Day Two:
The Anchorage and Torrent Bay
to Awaroa

AT THE NORTHERN END OF Torrent Bay, where the Coast Track cuts inland, is a cluster of holiday homes. The 3–4 hour walk between here and Bark Bay, contained within the watershed of the Falls River, is considered the most demanding part of the Coast Track. As always, the idea is to give yourself ample time in which to complete it and to walk at your own pace. The native forest you will encounter today is unsurpassed anywhere along this coastline.

Presently, from a high point on the track overlooking the sea, an attractive, crescent-shaped cove can be seen. This is Frenchman Bay; precisely who the Frenchman was is not known. The only access to the beach here is by sea.

Soon you arrive at the swing-bridge spanning the Falls River — the

Below: Frenchman Bay inlet.

Right: On the swing-bridge spanning the Falls River, trampers
pause to look at the river or to take photographs.

most significant and the most visibly arresting waterway on the Coast Track. The river spills into the sea at Sandfly Bay, near Pinnacle Island. There are two possible explanations for the name of this particular river. The first explanation is that it is named after the falls themselves and the second is that it is so named due to the fact that the river falls more than 1000 m in a mere 10 km. Either way, the upper reaches of the river are a steep, difficult terrain that prompted the notable mountaineer and explorer John Pascoe to comment in his book *A Land Uplifted High* that it is '... some of the roughest bush travelling I had yet to encounter'.

The second DOC hut on the south-to-north traverse of the Coast Track is at Bark Bay (containing 28 bunks) — a small, well-sheltered spot with good access to water. There are two campsites in the area.

The first European to settle here was Timothy Huffam, the father of four sons. Among the other ways they employed to make a living, the Huffams collected large amounts of bark (mostly rimu and beech) and shipped it to the Nelson tanneries where it was used in the tanning of hides. The family remained here until about 1904. The DOC hut was built on the site of the Huffams' homestead and the redwood trees near it date back to their time.

Remember to treat the Bark Bay inlet with caution. It too can be crossed with safety within 2–3 hours of the low water mark, but, at all other times, take the track which skirts the inlet.

Once again, the Coast Track will take you to fine stands of native timber before again returning to the coastline at Tonga Beach, or, as it is marked on the map, Tonga Quarry.

In the early 1900s, building-grade stone was cut from the granite cliffs at both ends of the beach: it was used in the construction of many buildings, most notably the former Central Post Office in Wellington, and the steps of Nelson Cathedral.

Across the Tonga Roadstead lies Tonga Island. The island and the surrounding sea (marked on maps and by markers on land) is a marine reserve and protects all marine life within its boundaries. Fishing and shellfish gathering are banned in this area. Little blue penguins, once common on the mainland, have sought sanctuary from predators on Tonga Island and seals are also found here.

Left: The Falls River, upstream of the swing-bridge.

Above: Bark Bay.

Left: Waterfall Creek, near Bark Bay.

The nearby beach at Onetahuti is first glimpsed from the Coast Track from a forest-clad high point. The beach looks more than inviting! This beach is really a continuation of Tonga Beach, and, for that reason, is often referred to as 'Big Tonga'. The beach itself is a long beach and the Maori meaning of its name is 'sand to run along'. This is fair enough as you could work up a fair sort of gallop here.

A campsite is located near the southern end of the beach. It is safe to swim at Onetahuti and it makes a wonderful spot for camping out in the summer.

At the northern end of the beach, the Coast Track crosses Richardson Stream, which, like the estuaries, is subject to tidal pressure. This stream can be tricky to cross at times so, once again, treat it with caution. It can generally be crossed only within two hours either side of the low tide.

There is now a steep climb up to Tonga Saddle. The heavily-forested hinterland can be seen from here, and once over Tonga Saddle, it is a steep descent towards Awaroa Bay.

Below: Tonga Island, as seen from Tonga Quarry.

On reaching Awaroa, many trampers, even if they are not stopping there overnight, call in at the Awaroa Café and Lodge. There is backpacker accommodation here, as well as the guided walkers' accommodation, and on the edge of the estuary is the Awaroa hut (with 22 bunks) and campsite.

Two points of interest are Awaroa (meaning 'long view') and Venture Creek. After dropping down from Tonga Saddle, the Coast Track crosses the tidal Venture Creek and then skirts the far side of it to the bay itself. However, at low tide, it is possible to follow it downstream. The creek takes its name from the 19-ton scow *Venture*, which was built here in 1905 and now rests as a decaying hulk in the creekbed near the bay. (As a matter of interest, the largest boat ever built here was the 50-ton topsail schooner *Awaroa* in 1905.)

Back in 1900, Awaroa was the largest settlement on the coast, with 13 families living here, and their children attending the local school. By following the edge of the estuary, beyond the DOC hut, you will come to the site of the schoolhouse, which was last used in about 1932. Near here is also a rusting steam-engine that was used for crushing bark.

Below: Richardson Stream in the foreground, at the northern end of Onetahuti.

Above: At low tide, trampers are leaving Awaroa Hut, which is seen on the lower ground; the DOC 'Hut Warden' accommodation is seen above.

Below: Awaroa Inlet at low tide.

Day Three:
Awaroa to Totaranui to Wainui Carpark

WHEN THE TIDE IS out at Awaroa, the sand in the inlet is both firm and yet suspiciously giving under one's feet. There are seemingly hundreds of birds on display — mostly variable and pied oystercatchers.

On the morning of my third day, I was attempting to get close enough to a couple of variable oystercatchers with bright orange beaks and jet black bodies when my attention was drawn to movement at Awaroa Hut. A number of independent trampers were about to leave. A couple headed off in a southerly direction, while the other four started across the inlet. The only obstacles that faced them were one or two streams which, in flowing out to sea, meandered in no particular hurry between raised, sandy bars. I watched them ford the first stream and it was no more than knee-deep. Soon they reached the far side of the inlet, where the Coast Track recommenced, and the forest gobbled them up.

Looking about me on a lovely spring morning it was a tranquil scene. Danger? Not here. And yet when the tide turns and the sea surges in again, the overall picture at Awaroa Inlet changes both swiftly and dramatically. The water is deep now, and cross-currents are

Below: The branchlets of a mature rimu tree drape across a silver fern.

rife. This is the only spot on the Coast Track where no alternative track has been cut and the only option one has is to cross the inlet here at low tide and/or within 2 hours of that time.

Once Awaroa Inlet is behind you, it is a short tramp to Waiharakeke Bay (wai meaning 'stream' and harakeke meaning 'flax') where a campsite is located.

Between 1906 and 1909, a sawmill was in operation near the beach. From here on, the Coast Track follows the same route taken by a bush tramway used to transport logs to the sawmill.

At the northern end of Waiharakeke Bay is Ratakura Point, and beyond there is Goat Bay where, presumably, someone once farmed goats. Today, there are feral goats further inland.

Almost before you realise it, you have reached Skinner Point which is just off the Coast Track. From there the beach at Totaranui can be seen. It has been less than a 2-hour walk from Awaroa.

Below: A golden sweep of sand as you look south along Totaranui Beach towards Skinner Point.

As I have already said, Totaranui is the start or end of the Coast Track as far as many trampers are concerned. For the record, the 'guided walk' goes no further than this point. However, we will press on to the carpark at Wainui.

There are a number of short walks from Totaranui that are ideal for holidaymakers and less serious trampers. One such walk is on the Coast Track — the 40-minute tramp through fine native forest to Anapai Bay. The beach at Anapai Bay is contained by granite cliffs and is regarded as one of the most attractive on the Coast Track. This is a great spot to pitch your tent at the campsite and take advantage of the safe swimming.

From Anapai Bay, Mutton Cove is soon reached. The bay was farmed until 1955 and the jaded old macrocarpa trees, which provide the campsite with shelter, date back to long before that.

Between Mutton Cove and Whariwharangi Bay, the Coast Track heads inland to follow an old farm track that links both places.

Below: At the DOC Information Centre, Totaranui, an American tramper checks out her Abel Tasman Parkmap.

Separation Point

The sailors prowling about [on Separation Point] had discovered some abandoned huts from which they carried off various objects used by the natives. I spoke very seriously to them about this and threatened to punish very severely any one who in future might dare to take such liberties.

— Dumont D'Urville, 1827

A 30-MINUTE DETOUR FROM the Coast Track leads to the coastal landmass the Maori named Te Mata, meaning 'the headland'. They used it as a lookout point. Today this headland is known as Separation Point.

A steep track will take you down to the lighthouse. Early European settlers thought that this rocky foreshore was the best spot on the coast

Left: Waiharakeke Bay.

Below: Fur seals can be seen all year round at Separation Point. Further south, kayakers are likely to encounter them in various places along the coastline.

to catch snapper and groper. This is also a good place to see seals, gannets diving for fish, perhaps an odd penguin — and, sometimes, even dolphins slicing without effort through the water. It would be a shame to miss the attractions of Separation Point.

Back on the Coast Track proper, it is no time at all before Whariwharangi Bay looms up. The area was settled by John Handcock in about 1897. He built a two-storey homestead here, but from 1926 onwards, no one appears to have lived permanently in the homestead. They still ran stock out here and used the homestead as a base for stockmen until 1972, by which time it was in a derelict condition. Fortunately, it was restored in 1980, and today it is the DOC accommodation hut with 20 bunks, an open fire and lots of atmosphere. There is also a campsite located close to the homestead.

The last section of the Coast Track presses on to finish at the DOC Information Shelter at the Wainui Carpark, which is located at the end of McShanes Road. This roughly 3.5 km walk takes about 90 minutes. As with the first stretch of the Coast Track out of Marahau, this stretch of track does not accurately reflect what lies ahead for anyone starting out from this end of the Coast Track. Unfortunately, there is much gorse on the hills above Wainui Bay — something at odds with what a national park is all about.

Later on, when it is all over and the walk is behind you, you will sit back and reflect upon the delights of the Coast Track, with its sweeping coastline, its splendid beaches, its forested gullies, its magnificent birdlife and its fascinating estuaries.

Distances and Travelling Times

Travelling times are generous and allow for photography stops and rest breaks. These times and distances also apply if you are walking the track north-to-south. Please note that trampers should be aware of the tides and consult tide charts, as they can affect travelling times. There is no high water track at Awaroa.

Marahau to The Anchorage and Torrent Bay*
Distance 11–13 km   Time 4 hours
*This can take 1 hour extra to Torrent Bay.

The Anchorage and Torrent Bay to Bark Bay
Distance 7–9 km   Time 2–2.5 hours

Bark Bay to Onetahuti
Distance 5–6 km   Time 1.5–2 hours

Onetahuti to Awaroa
Distance 5 km   Time 1.5 hours

Awaroa to Totaranui
Distance 5.5 km   Time 1.5–2 hours

Totaranui to Whariwharangi Hut
Distance 7.5 km   Time 3.5 hours

Whariwharangi Hut to Wainui Carpark
Distance 5.5 km   Time 1.5 hours

Above: Split Apple Rock — a local scenic attraction
as seen from the Abel Tasman Explorer.

Below: Another photograph shot from the Abel Tasman Explorer —
seals at rest on Tonga Island inside the Tonga Island Marine Reserve.

Practicalities

Sea-transport Options

Two water-taxi companies offer scenic cruises, day walk options and backpacker transport to various points along the Coast Track:

Abel Tasman Water Taxis
Private Bag Riwaka
Nelson
Telephone/fax: (03) 528-7497
Free phone: 0800 423-397

Abel Tasman Aquataxis Seafaris
Marahau Valley Road
RD2 Marahau
Telephone: (03) 527-8083
Free phone: 0800 278-282
Fax: (03) 527-8282

Sea Kayaking

Sea kayaking is a popular form of travel on the Abel Tasman Coast Track as a sleek and stable kayak allows visitors to explore the coastal environment and gives them access to some of the sheltered coves that the walking track bypasses. There are a number of companies operating in the area that offer rental of sea kayaks with options for independent or guided paddling in double or single kayaks. There is also the possibility for combining walking and kayaking, over one or several days. Most companies offer personalised programmes, with paddling distances being determined by weather conditions and levels of personal fitness.

The following kayaking companies have DOC approved concessions:

Abel Tasman Kayaks Ltd
Marahau Beach
RD2 Motueka
Free phone: 0800 527-8022
Fax: (03) 527-8032

Kahu Kayaks
147 Old Coach Road
Mahana
Upper Moutere
Telephone: (03) 543-2727

Kaiteriteri Kayaks
PO Box 309
Motueka
Telephone: (03) 527-8383

Kiwi Kayaks Ltd
PO Box 1556
Nelson
Free phone: 0800 695-494

Natural High
52 Rutherford Street
Nelson
Telephone: (03) 546-6936
Fax: (03) 546-6954
E-mail: chris@naturalhigh.co.nz
Website: www.seakayaknewzealand.com

Ocean River Adventure Company
Marahau Beach
RD2 Motueka
Telephone: (03) 527-8266
Free phone: 0800 732-529
Fax: (03) 527-8032
Website: www.seakayaking.co.nz

Planet Earth Adventures
Tennyson Street
Pohara
Takaka
Telephone: (03) 525-9095
E-mail: nigelm@clear.net.nz

Southern Exposure
71B Tahunanui Drive
Nelson
Telephone: (03) 546-4038

The Abel Tasman Adventure Co.
PO Box 1271
Nelson
Telephone: (03) 548-5835

The Sea Kayak Company NZ Ltd
506 High Street
Motueka
Telephone: (03) 528-7251

Please note:
Sea-kayaking with Abel Tasman National Park Enterprises at Awaroa Lodge has DOC
approval.

Tramping Gear

*The Abel Tasman Coast Track is not a 'typical New Zealand tramp' —
in many respects it is easier and closer to civilisation than most backcountry tramping routes. Perhaps for this reason it seems to attract a
significant number of people unnecessarily over-equipped or foolishly
under-equipped.*

— A Dennis, *A Park of All Seasons*

THE COAST TRACK RECEIVES around 2200 hours of sunlight
annually, among the highest in the country. This is a subtropical
region, so rainfall is also abundant. At Totaranui the annual rainfall
is about 1800 mm — twice the amount of rainfall in Nelson City.
Some items of clothing that you would take on a high-altitude track
are not required.

Above: Independent trampers on the Coast Track. They appear to be well equipped. Almost three times more people walk the Coast Track in a single year than walk the Milford or Routeburn tracks.

Recommended Gear for Independent Trampers Using DOC Huts and Campsites

Pack everything in four or five large plastic bags, then put these in one large, heavy-duty bag inside your pack. This way, even in torrential rain, you'll arrive in camp with everything dry.

Essentials
Frame pack
Make sure it is top quality only, and is roomy and comfortable.
Sleeping bag
Low-altitude models are satisfactory as down-filled bags might be too hot.
Sleeping mat/groundsheet/sheet of polythene
Nylon tent
A 1.5 x 2 m tent is okay for two people.

Clothing
Underwear
Socks
Wear one pair of thick woollen socks over a thin cotton pair if possible. Carry three spare pairs.
T-shirt/skivvy
Cotton is fine for most of the year.
Polypropylene is suggested for when walking in the colder months.
Personal preference dictates whether you want to wear polypropylene or cotton undergarments around camp.
Long trousers
Tracksuit bottoms are a good choice, easy to walk in and comfortable around camp.
Peaked cap
Woollen hats are not needed during the spring or summer.
Woollen sweater or fibrepile garments
Whatever the season, you must have some warm clothing with you.
Footwear — lightweight boots, running shoes or sneakers.
They are all suitable. Carry a spare pair of old sneakers for use in camp.
Waterproof jacket
A must.

Whatever you choose to carry, remember that it is essential that you have a complete change of dry clothing to slip into when you reach camp. Also, don't sit about in wet or damp gear as it's bad for you!

Cooking Utensils
Lightweight cooker with fuel
2 billies
(1 small and 1 medium.)
Frypan
Good for a variety of uses.
Plastic plate and mug; knife, fork and spoon set

Miscellaneous
Toiletries and a towel
First-aid kit
Small torch
Start out with new batteries.
Map
Parkmap Abel Tasman, Fourth Edition, the Department of Conservation, 1995. This can be obtained from many outlets but, if you have any difficulty, please contact: Terralink Map Centre, Private Bag 903, Upper Hutt.
Matches
Camera
Check batteries before leaving/carry a spare set.
Take ample film.
Sunglasses, sunscreen, lip protection and insect repellent
All are essential.
Small folding knife
A Leatherman super tool, with 10 locking blades (for various uses), which can also be worn in a pouch on your belt, is very versatile.
Optional
Swimming gear.
Cards, paperback book and writing materials.

Food
You'll use up heaps of calories on this track so high-energy food is essential if you want to feel at your best. Weight is a factor, so go for pasta, rice, oats, muesli, dehydrated vegetables, and consider some of the wide range of pre-cooked meals ideal for backpackers. For quick snacks and emergency rations, take chocolate, raisins, muesli bars, nuts, or a tasty combination of these, called scroggin. Remember to drink plenty of fluid. Also note that Giardia has been found in park waters so do not drink from streams. Boil all drinking and cooking water or treat with an additive available from pharmacies or DOC offices.

Abel Tasman National Park Enterprises
The Guided Walk and Abel Tasman Explorer

As much as I enjoy the mountains I find Abel Tasman National Park to contain all the elements of a truly great New Zealand holiday, enjoyable at any time of the year. With its unique seaside walkway, clear waters, unspoilt environment and idyllic golden sand bays, it gives rise to a wide range of habitats encouraging a diversity of flora and fauna. It's easy to understand why New Zealand's Conservation Department considers this one of the country's world ranking great walks. The Wilson Family is to be commended for the blend of history, character and comfort in their lodges.

— Sir Edmund Hillary

THE WILSON FAMILY HAS been associated with the coastline of the Abel Tasman since the 1870s. Operating under the name Abel Tasman National Park Enterprises, it offers a 3 or 5-day 'guided' package between Marahau and Totaranui. The guided walk may begin at either end of the track, and a trip in its own launch, the *Abel Tasman Explorer* (also used by independent trampers), is offered at either the start or the finish of the walk.

For those with time to spare, I strongly suggest the five-day trekking and kayaking option. This choice allows an extra night to be spent at its two accommodation houses on the track. Apart from kayaking, there is time to relax and to go swimming (summer only), or take a 'guided' walk to the Falls River region while based at Torrent Bay.

The first accommodation house is a superior holiday lodge at Torrent Bay. This lodge has been the Wilson family home for more than 30 years. The second house is at Awaroa, where the Wilsons first took up land. It is a stunning replica of the original homestead, Meadowbank, built by William Hadfield in 1884. Both houses feature hot showers, twin bedrooms, a drying room, an open fire and plenty of living space. They have a 'good feel' about them and the meals provided are excellent.

For more information about the Guided Walk or the Abel Tasman Explorer including timetables, please contact:

Abel Tasman National Park Enterprises
265 High Street
PO Box 351
Motueka
Nelson
Telephone: (03) 528-7801
Free phone: 0800 223-582
Fax: (03) 528-6087
E-mail: info@abeltasman.co.nz
Website: www.abeltasman.co.nz

Left: A party of day-trippers and trampers from the Abel Tasman Explorer coming ashore at Kaiteriteri.

Photographic Notes

AS MUCH AS ANY of the Department of Conservation's Great Walks, the Abel Tasman Coast Track lends itself beautifully to photography.

For general photographic purposes such as snapshots for your photo album or whatever, I suggest you use a 100 ASA or a 200 ASA print film, either Kodak or Fuji. While I prefer a 100 ASA film, a 200 ASA film is more suitable for overcast conditions and poor-lighting situations. I also suggest that when taking a shot you try to support the body of your camera in some way, as the results will be better.

I carried two Nikon F-301 bodies (a model no longer made) with me on the Coast Track. In order to keep my weight to a bare minimum, I used only two lenses — a 35–70 mm and a 200 mm lens (both Nikkor). My tripod was a lightweight Slik U-8000. Although some of the wildlife shots presented here were taken at the time, the majority were shot at different locations using more powerful telephoto lenses (300–400 mm).

With the exception of the front cover, all of the photographs in this book were taken with Fujichrome 100 ASA Provia film.

Left: Watching the moon rise over Torrent Bay.

Selected Reading

Dennis, A, *A Park of All Seasons: The Story of Abel Tasman National Park*, New Zealand Lands and Survey, Wellington, 1985.

Burton, R, and Atkinson, MA, *A Tramper's Guide to New Zealand's National Parks*, Reed Methuen, Auckland, 1987.

Host, E, *The Enchanted Coast*, J McIndoe, Dunedin, 1976.

Moore, C, *New Zealand Wilderness Walks*, Hodder Moa Beckett, Auckland, 1996.

Pickering, M, and Smith, R, *101 Great Tramps in New Zealand*, new edition, Reed, Auckland, 1998.

Potton, C, *Classic Walks of New Zealand*, Craig Potton Publishing, Nelson, 1997.

Temple, P, *The BP Guide to the Abel Tasman Coast Track*, Penguin Books, Auckland, 1989.

Wild New Zealand, Reader's Digest, Sydney, 1981.

Map: Parkmap Abel Tasman, Fourth Edition, Department of Conservation, 1995.